A Different Key

A Different Key
John Mole

NEW WALK EDITIONS
Leicester • Nottingham

ACKNOWLEDGMENTS

Some of these poems have previously appeared in *The Spectator* and *The Rialto*.

Copyright © John Mole 2017

John Mole has asserted his right under Section 77
of the Copyright, Designs and Patents Act 1988 to be
identified as the sole author of this work.

Published by New Walk Editions
c/o Rory Waterman,
Department of English, Media and Creative Cultures,
Nottingham Trent University, NG11 8NS
and
c/o Nick Everett, Centre for New Writing,
University of Leicester, LE1 7RH
www.newwalkmagazine.com

Contents

The Rebuke	7
Comma	8
A Premonition	9
A Granddaughter's Farewell	10
Folk Festival in a Churchyard	11
On a Line from David Holbrook	12
Drought	13
The Hip	14
Piano Man	16
Hacked	18
The Humpty Dumpty Stamp-Licker	19
Fraught	20

The Rebuke

Driven by language, as a pianist
By the sight of ivories, and restless
When not at the keyboard
Improvising word after word
To discover myself, I seldom
Held back. Poetry was the momentum
And melody of my being,
Always either on song or clearing
My throat for it. Arpeggios
In search of resolution, one phrase
Chasing another, the delight
Of never having to wait
For voice or accompaniment
To find its match in the imminent
And likely poem
                Which is why now
In bereavement's wake, the undertow
Of loss, I fear the doldrum drift
From one false start to another, to be left
Behind by what was once
The creative certainty of chance
That drove me. When I look
At what I have written, its rebuke
Is that such conscious effort
Should seem so lifelessly apart
From impulse, that such wordiness
Should seek for reassurance, and that loss
Has yet to lighten, finding the way
To make fresh music in a different key.

Comma

Not a boomerang or a frisbee thrown
in the expectation of return
but a careless comma loosed mid-air
on a breezy page, insouciant,
experimental, to see how it flies
and where it lands, the fresh ground
chanced upon, choosing not to settle
any place it has before. Or otherwise
the deliberate one that made his day
for Oscar Wilde when he removed it
from a sentence, telling lunchtime friends
that this had been his morning's work,
then meeting them again for dinner,
celebrating after he had put it back.

A Premonition
i.m. Edward Thomas

Who was it that cleared his throat
To what end? With something to say
Before he thought the better of it
And settled back in the only way

Of being a ghost? Let birdsong,
Risen above all incidental sounds,
Leave its crescendo with the living
As music is a wordlessness which mends.

Besides, what would be broken
Other than his heart by hearing said
All that he could utter of those men,
His travelling companions, the dead

He now belonged with? Life
Best left for those with time to dream
Their onward journey, and grief
A bare platform, a hiss of steam.

A Granddaughter's Farewell

On her grandmother's coffin
Along with wreaths and photographs
Left by the family, she'd asked
To be allowed to place there
Her own offering for the journey.
And so this seven-year-old's request
Was granted, but what amazed
All those who knew her best
And who expected a favourite toy,
Was how with due solemnity
She'd added to the tributes
A card without embellishment—
No drawing of her Gran
Or of the two of them together
But just those five familiar words
Keep Calm and Carry On.

Folk Festival in a Churchyard
for Kenneth Padley

Shadows there on the flint wall,
Ink-black silhouettes much
Larger than in life, reach
Out to each other. Who can tell

That light is not playing tricks
Or that a well-aimed beam
Has not now usurped the moon
And the hands of the church clock

Gone into reverse? These
Could all be ghosts relieved
Of their whiteness, the loved,
The lost, returned to praise

This annual gathering—
Stranger, neighbour, friend
Who wander on sacred ground
To drink and dance and sing.

On a Line from David Holbrook
'To watch pass by a thundering old Dad'
('Mother Nature, Mother Time')

There are lines that stick around like this one
For a lifetime, singly tenacious when the rest
Have been forgotten, wonderful enough
To start me searching among faded pages
For the freshness of discovery, that sudden recognition,
Even a moment's urge to pass it off as mine.

Poet of married love and family, it took your death
To send me back to where this came from, found
The year I met my wife, before our children
Raced ahead of me and into poems that outgrew
The need for imitation. In time we all pass by,
Bound to whatever watches us and steals our thunder.

Drought

The cracked face of exhaustion
Is not that of an old friend
Gone finally to earth. It stares up

From the bed it lies on,
A familiar stranger
Thirsty for water and love.

The Hip

    after Gogol and Ian Crichton Smith
    for Peter Scupham

The hip set off down the street
Bright as a new pin
High on titanium
And in the groove,
An exemplary dancing-master
Tripping fantastic light.

How it leapt in its socket
To unheard melodies
Without recoil
Or a jarring sound.

This, it exclaimed,
Makes the world my cakewalk
And a foxtrot miracle
All the way.

Now it could easily
Set the ball rolling
And skip to the loo
Down slippery steps,

Its progress the envy
Of passers by
Who stopped to admire
Such a perfect fit.

Hip hip hooray
Cried a wag in his cups
Both legless and witless,
Walk on, walk on!

And so with never
A soft-shoe shuffle
But the new-found glory
Of twinkling toes,
The hip hopped away
And around a corner
Where life lay in wait
For the dance to begin.

Piano Man
Oscar Peterson, Montreux 1977

Heavyweight but handy
With the glissandi,
On a held chord he lingers
Until the spread of those fingers
Contracts to a thumb
And he starts his run.

From a counterpoint fugue he
Breaks into boogie
And torrential sweat
But you ain't heard nothing yet.
Now suddenly gentle,
Blue and sentimental.

Athlete of jazz,
His racy razzmatazz
From hot to cool
Breaks every rule
But he knows that his act is
Perfected by practice.

The audience roars
And he rides its applause
To the finishing line
Then, taking his time,
He gets up to bow
As he wipes his brow.

Passion, skill, wit—
This has been it,
The perfect balance
Of thought and chance,
Jazz with a grin,
Spaced out, reined in.

And so he stands,
Those miraculous hands
Joined together there
As if in prayer
But now what they do
Is say *Thank you. Thank you!*

HACKED

Find the body where it fell.
All is very far from well.
This is a story that will sell.

No time to take a second look.
Fresh bait dangles from the hook.
Someone must be brought to book.

Messages remain unread.
Listen in on them instead,
Postscript echoes of the dead.

Search the neighbourhood for a clue,
Fact or fiction? It's down to you.
Any subterfuge will do.

Gather reports and hold the page.
Release them slowly stage by stage.
Suspects, friends, their sex, their age.

This is a story that has sold.
Now for the next plot to unfold.
Grief is worth its weight in gold.

The Humpty Dumpty Stamp-Licker

Yellow legs akimbo, slapping fat thighs,
Perched on a water-drum with two pop eyes,
When you twist the cap on its porcelain crown
This ridiculous egg won't tumble down
But sticks out its tongue from a mouth so wide
That it almost splits the shell from side to side,
Then you twist again, the tongue goes in
And leaves you with the open wound of a grin.
It sat on my grandfather's writing desk,
No less functional than grotesque,
But now it's on mine by inheritance,
Watching me write. Throw it out? Not a chance.
I know that its dried-up uselessness
Is a bond between us that we daren't express.
There's a look of horror on its painted face,
Its parched tongue gags and stays in one place,
Its water drum is empty, its bulbous head
Twists to no purpose, becoming instead
A sort of eccentric memento mori
As we gaze at each other, eye to eye,
Waiting for an envelope that will not stick
With nothing inside and no stamp to lick.

Fraught

is how I look, he tells me,
sounding the fricative of a fierce
emphatic concern. I thank him
for his candour though preferring
this consolation from a friend
who says *When I saw you
arriving at the door
the words that came to mind
were 'trim' and 'buoyant'.*

How am I coping? Am I eating,
taking care, managing alone
and looking after myself?
The interrogation of a hand
laid too lightly on the shoulder
or upper arm, those gestures
that make of me a man apart,
how I welcome yet resent
the mild, compassionate intrusion.

But does it help me at all
to write like this? Probably not
so to those who have read thus far
I give you leave to go,
as I shall now, about the business
of getting on with things,
making the best of what remains
for everyone, trim and bouyant,
back on the beat and utterly unfraught.